POETRAITS & THOUGHT

By Thomas MacCalla

Print information available on the last page.

Rev. date: 03/08/2019

To order additional copies of this book, contact:
Xlibris
1-888-795-4274
www.Xlibris.com
Orders@Xlibris.com

TABLE OF CONTENTS

DEDICATION

To Jacqueline Caesar MacCalla
& William Adorno
Best of Family and Friends

PREFACE

Poetraits and Thought is a poetic display of beauty in various forms. **Poetraits** are visual verse renderings similar to those presented in *Artistry in Word Music* (2014) and *Inside the Muse* (2017). **Thought** refers to narrative reflections on the present, speculation on the emerging future, and fantasy on the seemingly impossible.

EXPERIENCE THE POEM

Envision poetry as word music
visualizing thoughts and emotions,
to reproduce silent songs of the mind.

Listen to the measured beat of the muse
maintaining the rhythm of melodies
for the flow of insights and life lyrics.

Feel the warmth of the verbal visuals
and the possibilities of meaning
with the power of imagination

Experience that artistic moment
by recreating the poet's intent
and offering your interpretation.

PART 1

Poetraits

Poetraits are visual verse renderings of natural beauty in various forms. **Thought** refers to discourse on the present, our emerging future, and the seemingly impossible.

BEING

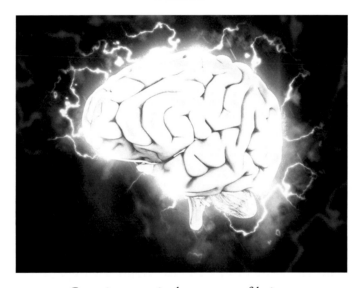

Consciousness is the essence of being,
aware of self and perceiving outside,
and we live in the Planet of the Mind.

We possess an invisible spirit
that is part of One Universal Mind
in a perpetual energy field.

OCTOGENARIAN CONSCIOUSNESS

When we hear footsteps in our later years
we are more conscious of fleeting time.
and start reliving the past, with ask questions
about the choices made along the way,

We're curios about uncertainty
longevity, leisure, and afterlife
and try to put them into perspective,
knowing the answer are not forthcoming.

Unleash the restless spirit caged inside
and allow fantasy to chart a course
that leads to happiness and fulfillment
with unparalleled hope and sense of self.

Reset the clock and enjoy the moment
with the full measure of confidence
to be able to fathom the unknown
and discover the meaning of wholeness.

INNER VISION

Peer through the mind's eye
and probe deep inside
with inner vision.

Imaging seeing tomorrow today
with sunshine and hope

Envision a world
of togetherness
in pursuit of peace

Realize insight
as a special gift
of the open mind.

INSIGHT

Know today is yesterday's tomorrow
and we can make the day after better
by appreciating views of the world
that may be different from those we see.

Learning begins with curiosity
that leads to knowledge and discovery,
and questioning challenges tradition
as the undisputed measure of truth.

Ideas are considered opinions
based on evidence and intuition
and join together as threads of wisdom
like a string of peals shining with insight.

Welcome the new day of enlightenment
shedding light on the other side of doubt
to reveal the gift of understanding
and appreciate the freedom of thought.

BEYOND LOGIC

Logic deals with the reality of Now,
the probable and the possible,
disputing arguments for absolutes.

On the edge of reason is openness,
fertile ground for curiosity
where seeds of wishful thinking are planted.

Go beyond finite limits of logic
and envision an ethereal realm
permeating a boundless universe.

Let mindfulness and collective thought
stretch mentality's reach and recognize
incomprehensible is still real.

EDGE OF REASON

Create a realm on the edge of reason
where dreams and desires are possible
and the impossible seemingly real.

Listen to the soulful voice deep within
reinforcing belief in the unknown
and commitment to the unknowable.

Think of extraterrestrial life
and the prospect of living forever
with other spirits in an afterward.

LIGHT OF DAY

Instantly today becomes tomorrow,
echoing the silence of the moment
in the chamber of the now that we own.

Imagination bridges the unseen,
and allows us to fathom forever
despite the limits of logic and faith.

As we continue to search for meaning,
and await the everlasting promise,
we are plagued with uncertainty and doubt.

In the meantime enjoy love and freedom,
savoring memories of yesteryears
and pursuing the dreams we put on hold.

Praise the innocence in eyes of children,
aware of how time will steal it away
so they can discover truth on their own.

Listen to the tune of integrity
where we are true to ourselves and others,
and our belief systems find common ground.

BEYOND THE HORIZON

As the sun sinks below the water's edge,
We are heartened by knowing that it will return
As part of a pre-ordained ritual.

We often wonder about what lies beyond
The vast expanse above and depths below
And look forward to knowing more in time.
Those on the other side share the same view
And are curious about other worlds
Beyond the horizon of their water.

Embrace the unifying rays of light
Shining on our global connectedness
And work toward bridging our differences.

LONE TREE

The lone tree is not alone just different,
standing tall amongst predominant green peers
like a minority in the human field.

TRUISMS

Absolutes are pillars of certitude,
relativity. the shadow of truth,
curiosity the source of doubt
wonderment the testimony to hope.

Friendship is sharing oneself with someone
Logic is the artistry of reason
Faith is belief in the unknowable
and Love the sustainable source of life.

NEWNESS

Behold the radiant flowers of spring
reflect the beginning of something new
while stimulating a new sense of hope
with a floral welcome breath of beauty.

SLEEP TALK

Sometimes I feel like J. Alfred Prufrock,
wondering what I will or should do today,
then words advice surface from within
about gratitude for being alive.

Listen to a silent voice of the soul
speak about having a purpose in life
and feel the vibrations of consciousness
shake the window of resistance and doubt.

Awareness and ability to act
are the key elements of survival,
while acumen and past experience
are essential to achieving success.

The key to living a loving marriage
is unconditional sharing of self
with caring and willingness to forgive,
knowing you're growing together as one.

BEAUTY BY DESIGN

See beauty in the creative design
and the structural configuration
produce a portrait with concrete and glass
set on a hilltop as a centerpiece.

Sense the artistry of brick and mortar
with a prideful architectural pose
creating a new natural setting
in global metropolitan centers.

PART 2

Thought

Thought deals with collaboration for innovation and competitiveness in a digital world, the impact of technology on society and rise of the new era citizen. Part 2 is prefaced by poems on Thought Power, reflections in a **Minduverse** and the **Quantum Frontier.**

We live in a digital society impacted by advanced technology and the constant of change Some of the key elements in this environment are the Internet, Social Media, Cell Phones and the applications of autonomous systems. They influence the way we engage, connect, protect, explore, invest, and inspire.

Technology is an enabling tool that allows us to communicate and collaborate globally in real time, foster innovation and facilitate problem solving. Through advanced wireless, it enhances the capabilities of autonomous systems, making them extensions of the home, office, and workplace.

DIGITAL WORLD

We live in a digital world
preempting tomorrow today
with technology advances
that change lives at school, work, and play.

Mobile phones are ubiquitous,
connecting people globally,
unwittingly enslaving us
even though we feel in control.

Data is the foremost driver
collected to know and predict
as the digital big brother
and controller of decisions.

Think about the pros and the cons
and beware of devious minds
manipulating the machines
to diminish the common good.

THOUGHT POWER

The human mind enables consciousness,
fuels thinking, feeling and memory,
transmits thought as cosmic wave vibrations
with an invisible power of spirit
engaged with a higher order of thought.

Thought is the seeding ground of decisions
and powerful stimulant of the Will
analyzing alternative choices,
contemplating and guiding behavior
in anticipation of good results.

Thought power is the primary force of
ideas, intentions and desires.
manipulator of introspection
influenced by culture and tradition
and precious domain of the private self.

SEASONED THOUGHT

Time has a way of reaching
into our memory bank
to keep yesteryears alive
and sow new seeds for aging.

Time reaches into our memory bank
keeping the thoughts of yesteryears alive,
sowing seeds that develop with aging,
and reminding us of the tolling bell.

Curiosity is the source of life
enabling us to dream and to thrive
by making an investment in oneself
and share the bounty of relationships.

Navigate the currents of uncertainty
and continue the search for new knowledge
by being aware and doing what's right,
loving others and knowing you are loved.

COLLABORATION FOR INNOVATION AND COMPETITIVENESS

Collaboration and open resource sharing are essential for win-win and sustainable outcomes. Competitiveness spurs innovation and ensures success in the global marketplace by providing a formidable competitive and mutually beneficial advantage. Essentially collaboration is the process of establishing mutually beneficial and forging trusting relationships to solve common problems for the greater good. It is a form of teamwork that requires people to constructively explore their differences together to share and maximize limited resources to find solutions for desired outcomes.

Collaboration does not just happen. It has to be cultivated in order to infuse a spirit of togetherness and nurtured to seed the ground for the next generation of collaborators. It is a complex process that is unpredictable and goes beyond cooperation, and involves trust and a commitment to shared values that go beyond compliance.

Innovation refers to discovery, change and creative problem solving. It recognizes and capitalizes on opportunity, facilitates and accelerates advancement, and adds value. Innovation helps to shape near and long-range futures and improve the quality of life. Coupled with collaboration, it is a practical and effective means of spurring and spreading economic growth and development locally, regionally, nationally and globally.

The concept of Collaborative Competitiveness involves shared interest, trust, mutual respect, and confidentiality. It also implies the conversion of a "What is in it for me?" mindset into "What is in it for us?" for the common good. One of the main challenges for small and medium-sized businesses is being aware of and familiar with high performance computing to the extent that they can demonstrate their capacity to use cyber- infrastructure tools and be recognized by larger firms as competitive suppliers.

Another challenge is identifying, mapping, and internalizing a region's assets and complementary resource networks and be actively engaged, a dynamic communications system and resource network.

TECH THOUGHT

Connectivity and Information
are the grand masters of technology
and the Internet is Lord of the Land.

What matters most is who knows and who cares
that we are tech wise and cyber secure
and ready for the internet of Things.

Invest in new forms of tech engagement
to promote digital understanding
and empower all generations.

Foster the sense of caring and sharing,
collaboration for innovation,
and global outreach for social justice.

PROMISING THOUGHT

Peace and War are off-springs of love and hate,
inseparable foes and life companions
overshadowing the power of love.

Can we find a way to live together,
despite distrust of our differences,
greed, and pursuit of fortune at all cost.

Can we compromise for the common good,
even though tradition gets in the way
and respect and tolerance are footnotes.

Let's build a world order of harmony
with caring, sharing, empathy and trust
and eradicate global ignorance.

Let's focus on continuous learning,
and chart a new course of togetherness
with social justice and equality
as common bonds of world community.

INDIVIDUAL SELF AND SOCIALIZATION

To understand the role of citizen in a global society, it is important to have a sense of the person in his/her role as a human being, and as an unique individual. Recognizing that the relativity of cultural patterns and the influences of socialization on the way we think and behave will enable us to transcend our personal world and navigate global space.

Man's complex nature as a thinking, feeling, and acting member of homo sapiens must be viewed in relation to his role as a social animal (i.e. being aware of his/her existence as a member of a group and being socialized within a member of a family of significant others, as well as a community of influential and generalized others).

To reach the point of understanding the individual as a complex, whole person who has the potential to act as a socially-responsible individual, raises many questions about identity individualism, collectivism, public and private behavior, culture, and other relevant issues related to the citizen's role in community. Discussing these dimensions of the person helps us understand the dynamics of human interaction within the framework of a changing society and the broad spectrum of diverse cultures and communities.

Where does one begin to explore the concept of responsible citizenship amidst diversity and conflicting world views, environmental concerns, and uneven socioeconomic factors that tend to drive us further apart rather than bring us closer together? It seems most appropriate to start by building we first must build a framework for understanding the dynamics of human interaction between the person, community, and society-at-large.

Building such a framework must begin with a basic awareness of the person as a biological, psychological, cultural, and social being existing in an environment that provides the foundation for further growth and development. It also will prepare one to become a fully-functioning, positive role model for responsible citizenship.

WORLD VIEW

We live in an interdependent world, balancing
differences in people, perspectives, preferences and
persuasion

Identity, belonging, love, and pride are
human qualities and desires wrought by family
and discovery.

Though many live in lands of liberty,
opportunity and the rule of law, others are
subdued or impoverished.

Culture, tradition and belief systems shape
the character of community and the values that
govern behavior.

People should not be starving or homeless, deny
immigrants seeking to belong,
or thwart freedom of speech and assembly

May the sense of responsibility ignite
the spirit of brotherly love and inspire global
citizenship..

NEW ERA CITIZENSHIP

Technological advances and the persuasiveness of the Information Age challenges everyone to acknowledge the presence and demands of citizens in an interdependent global community. We also need to be cognizant of the fact that the shift from a nation-state world view to a global outlook requires major adjustments to the inherent values and historical, social, and economic practices of the more traditional society.

The evolutionary spiral that drives change has been accelerated and efforts to recalibrate have been tempered by the pressures of time and politics. As social philosopher Bernard Dauenhauer articulated in Citizenship in a Fragile World, the role of citizenship in the global community is complex. It goes beyond borders and requires education for all ages in dealing with foreign states and their peoples. The new citizen needs to be more tolerant of differences, aware of global issues, be flexible in adjusting to change in work, family and community settings, and be comfortable with ambiguity, and recognize their role in contributing to the well-being of others through reasonable and responsible behavior.

In short, the new Information Age citizen must embrace the world in altruistic terms and recognize the connectivity to everyone and everything in a global context. We need to acknowledge differences and collaborate to share commonality is the new social imperative. We also must recognize that our fragile ecosystem is in trouble and we are tasked by default to forge new community realities that bridge boundaries and go beyond the limits of cultural convention and the perceived world of nation states. The end game is a community renewal process based on inclusiveness and togetherness.

QUERIES

What if? So What? and Who Cares? Are questions
that stir the mind in search of answers
hiding in shadows, doubt, or out of reach.

What is the truth were wrapped in a garb of lies
out of innocence or by design,
should we not stand up, speak out, and counter?

So What? is a testament of concern
that requires the disclosure of facts
to avoid any misunderstanding.

Who Cares? Is a symbol of integrity
that values commitment to honoring
honesty, fairness, and belonging.

Collectively, these queries enable
the pursuit of wisdom and good judgment,
overriding doubt and indifference.

MINDUVERSE AND QUANTUM FRONTIER

The Minduverse is a replica of an intelligent cosmos with a universal consciousness.

The Quantum Frontier refers a boundless dynamic sphere interconnected and inseparable energy patterns, the most potent of which is **Thought.**

Thought consists of cosmic waves that penetrate all time and space. Also noteworthy are the observations of researcher at Cambridge, Princeton, and the Max Planck Institute for Physic who regard consciousness as living in a quantum state after death and quantum mechanic predicting some version of "life after death". Underscoring these remarks is the statement by Hans-Peter Durr, former head of the Max Planck Institute for Physics in Munich, claiming that the brain stores wave function information to be uploaded into a spiritual quantum field.

WANDER IN WONDER

Envision trillions of stars in the sky
and other forms with intelligent life
connected to a cosmic consciousness.

With the power of the mind and spirit
explore a limitless quantum frontier
in an orderly chaotic vacuum.

Now dive into the depth of inner space
with an enhanced sense of the private self and
find clues to unraveling the unknown.

Travel in wonderment with confidence
appreciating the great gift of life
and the inheritance of love and hope.

DYNAMIC SPACE

We are humans made of the stuff of stars
in dynamic space with dark energy
engulfed in a limitless cosmic field
of intelligent, orderly chaos.

Outer space is not empty, nor a void,
but a vacuum of vibrating waves
in a perpetual energy field
where everything is interconnected.

With continued cosmic expansion
our known universe may not be unique
but one of many beyond the dark edge
and possibly we may not be alone.

New knowledge through advanced technology
suggest a rethinking of the cosmos
as random evolvement from a big bang
and prospect of creation from nothing.

QUANTUM FRONTIER

We live our mind, consciously aware
of the self and external environs
wondering who we are, and why wc are her.

Journey with me through the quantum frontier
of which we all are an integral part
and everything is interconnected.

Listen to the silent voices within
discuss meaning and rationalize faith
sensing a neural link to the cosmos.

Explore a Minduverse with thought power
in a perpetual energy field
tuned to cosmic vibration frequencies.

Feel the release of the new inner self
enter the domain of a conscious cosmos
and follow the guiding light of One Mind.

Use the power of imagination
to envision a spiritual world
and communion with those who once were.

PART 3

Poster Poems

Poster poems are "Poetraits" displaying visual verse renderings with companion Photo art captioned with lines of poetry. The following collection focuses on the universality of beauty and the perceptions of Nature's artistry.

POETRY OF THE OUTDOORS

Welcome to poetry of the outdoors,
Where Nature's artistry is on display
In the fields of Scotland and Tahoe Blue

BEAUTY IN THE OPEN

View the clear beauty of openness
in the expanse of ocean and desert
portraying the still art of the heavens.

TREE LINES

Trees salute the sky with a command presence
and stand as sentinels on the walkways
awaiting the applause of onlookers.

LANDSCAPES

See the vast expanse of the Grand Canyon
expose the landscape of an ancient sea
and behold the beauty of Erin's Cliffs of Mohr

RAINBOW COLORS

Autumn leaves sparkle with seasonal colors
like colorful streaking stripes in a rainbow
parading along with the clouds in the sky.

NATURAL BEAUTY

Nature paints poetry in the open
as a heavenly expression of art
with Lake Lucerne and an Alpine Meadow
portrayed on an invisible canvas.

BIRD ROCKS

Brown wooden bird surveying the vast ocean
with a commanding look and prideful presence
personifying the meaning of control.

Piles of stones are leaning on one another
as solid rock guardians of the shoreline
symbolizing power with a stoic stance.

SEASONAL MOODS

Witness the colorful parade of trees
facing the autumn viewer's stand with pride
and yielding to the frost of winter white.

WATER IMPRESSIONS

See picturesque views of Nature's seascapes
in coastal waterfalls of Ireland
and shores of Italy's Costa Brava.

WATER WILDERNESS

Sierra and Swiss water wilderness
reproduce the artistry of Nature
as natural renderings of beauty.

PART 4

The Music Room

Welcome to the Music Room and listen to the sounds of word music. and lyrics as poetry. Enjoy sound clips from talented music makers Reuben Alexander and Sylvia MacCalla Moore.

Get in step with *Take It Easy* and *I Can't Stop.* Relax with *You Make me Smile* and keep on moving with *Put Some Love On It.* The Music Room session ends with the lyrics of my song.

TAM'S SONG

Poetry is word music with a beat,
a composition of the heart and mind
played with notes of measured syllables
and in rhythm with the cadence of the thought

END NOTE

Some memories of yesteryear still make us smile when certain thoughts are triggered. Remember when school, the play ground, and neighborhood were the whole wide world? And what about those odd occasions when relatives came for a short visit and seemed to stay forever.

Recently, I was looking at pictures of my parents, Esther, mother and household business woman and daddy or Doc, the down-to-earth dentist who worked out of his home office and private dental lab. I also reminisced about brother Al, whom we called the original Salt of the Sea and Eric, the talented artist waiting for a call from New York. Instantly, sayings and indelible incidents came into view.

I can still hear Lady Esther say "Thomas clean your room and don't make so much noise. When I climbed the stairs in our sixteen-room home, I heard Uncle Sinclair in my head bellowing: "Thomas, pick up your feet."

Then there were school day and boot camp training recalls. What was in my favor was stubbornness and the feeling that I was capable of doing anything.

Though physically small in stature, I insisted on playing the center position on the football team and thought I deserved to be the point guard on the basketball team and rejection didn't bother me.

Also in my favor was the doting love of my sisters Ruby and Hazel, the mild mannered attention of my brother Eric and protective force of my brother Alfred and his friends Richard Hamilton and Charlie Beal. It made me somewhat blind to and a good candidate for the Marine Corps despite just meeting the minimum height and weight requirements. The side that I kept to myself was playing with words and writing poetry without learning how.

Of particular note was my brazenness out of ignorance. Upon arriving and reporting to the Second Battalion, Fifth Marines during the Korean War, I had to stand in line for Regimental Review. Being somewhat of an oddity as the first African American in the Corps to get a command, I was in the front row.

The Colonel walked up and down the aisle and when he came to me and stopped. He said, "Is it Mac Calla or Mac Caula" and without thinking, I said, "Take your pick sir." Hell burst onto the scene with the retort, "Who do you think you're talking too?" I melted with a humble look of apology and was marked man, immediately receiving orders to go to the front lines and patrol in front of the lines at the UN Panmunjon Peace Talks.

The incident was akin to my earlier life as a student under Jesuit Rule. Because my brother Eric was a track start, I went out for the track team at Prep School. I knew that I would not make it, but I had to try. I remember running round and round and was ready to stop until I heard the coaching good priest say, keep running until I tell you to stop. Fortunately, I fell from exhaustion and heard him say "Good, Thomas," you can get up now and get dressed. It was then that the motto "always faithful" became part of me.

Printed in the United States
By Bookmasters